Conceived and produced by
Lionheart Books
10 Chelmsford Square
London NW10 3AR

Editor Lionel Bender,
assisted by Madeleine Samuel
Designer Ben White

From an original idea by
Lionel Bender and Dr. J. F. Oates.
Primatologist. Hunter College.
New York

Adapted and first published in
the United States in 1987
by Silver Burdett Press.
Morristown. New Jersey.

*Library of Congress Cataloging in
Publication Data*

Stidworthy, John, 1943–
   Tiger.

   (A Year in the life)
   Includes index.
   Summary: Describes a year in the life
of a female Indian tiger who lives on the
edge of a forest.
   1. Tigers—Juvenile literature.
(1. Tigers)
I. Title.   II. Barrett, Priscilla, ill.
III. Series
QL737.C23S74 1987 599.74'428
86-31425
ISBN 0-382-09444-1
ISBN 0-382-09454-9 (pbk.)

A YEAR IN THE LIFE: TIGER
Written by John Stidworthy
Illustrated by Priscilla Barrett

ABOUT THIS BOOK

Our book tells the story of the life of one particular tiger over a single year. We have written and illustrated our story as if we had watched the tiger's behavior through the year, noticing how its activities changed at different periods. By looking closely at one tiger, we give you a good understanding of how an individual animal reacts to others and to the conditions it experiences in the wild.

We have called our tiger Mohini. On pages 4 and 5 we show you where Mohini lives and tell you a little about Mohini's habits and lifestyle. Our main story, on pages 6 to 29, follows a year in Mohini's life, and is divided up into six sections between one and three months long. Each section begins with a large illustration showing the environment and one aspect of Mohini's behavior at that time. The following two pages in each section continue our main story and show some of Mohini's other activities during the same period. On page 30 we discuss tiger conservation.

INTRODUCTION

Tigers are the largest members of the cat family. All types of cat have the same body build and behavior. They are usually solitary stealthy hunters, making use of camouflage to creep up on an animal before making a final rush to knock it down and kill it. They have keen forward-facing eyes, allowing them to judge distances accurately when hunting. Their hearing is good and their sense of smell adequate, being used more in social behavior than in hunting. They can pull back their claws inside sheaths between their toes, and can walk silently on the pads of their paws. All cats are powerful animals and can leap and accelerate well, but cannot run far without tiring.

All types of cat have 28 teeth. The front teeth are small but sharp and used for grooming or making a nip in the skin of prey. Next are the huge fangs, the killing weapons. The cheek or side teeth are used to slice off lumps of meat to swallow.

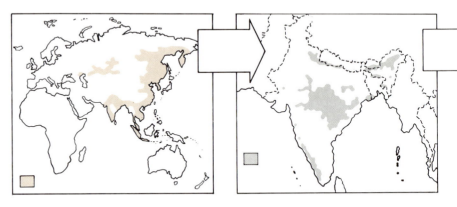

△ Tigers, Latin name *Panthera tigris*, live in Asia and range from Siberia south to Sumatra but are not found on high mountains. The most southerly tigers tend to be the smallest and darkest in color.

△ The Indian subcontinent holds the greatest number of tigers in the world. This book is about tigers in an area of central India with hills and forest and also some open grassland.

Mohini – an Indian tiger

Tigers vary in size from place to place. An Indian tiger can grow over 9 feet long from nose to end of tail, about 36 inches tall and weigh 440 pounds. Siberian tigers are the biggest and reach over 12 feet long. Males are usually larger than females, and have a neck ruff. In the wild, tigers live about 12 years. They are adult at three or four years. Our tiger, Mohini, is a six-year-old female living in central India.

The seasons

In Mohini's home area it is generally warm. In the middle of winter, though, it can be cool. In summer it is hot and there is much rain. In this, the monsoon season, the vegetation is lush and green. In winter there is little or no rain. Deciduous trees shed their leaves during cool late winter. They remain leafless and bare until early summer. The changing climate affects the tigers because their prey move between forest and grassland with the seasons.

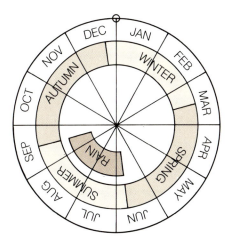

△ The calendar in Mohini's home area. A small calendar is used in the main story to show the time span of each section.

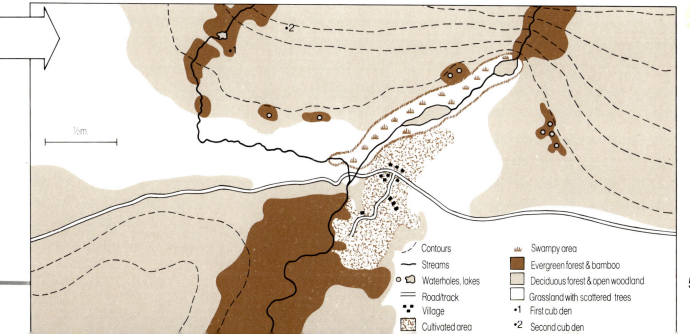

Legend	
Contours	Swampy area
Streams	Evergreen forest & bamboo
Waterholes, lakes	Deciduous forest & open woodland
Road/track	Grassland with scattered trees
Village	•1 First cub den
Cultivated area	•2 Second cub den

½m.

5

THE RAINS FINISH

It was early morning. The forest was quiet except for the sounds of insects. Mohini lifted her head and roared briefly. No answer came.

Mohini had just finished a large meal. She and her cub had been feeding on a nilgai antelope. The cub was full too, but still picked at the carcass. The two tigers had fed well in the last few weeks, going into the grassland at night to stalk the herds of grazing animals that gathered there during the rainy season. During the day the tigers retreated into the forest away from the heat of the sun. When they made a kill they usually pulled the carcass into cover before starting the feast. When they had eaten enough they moved away, but if there was still meat on the carcass they returned to it for several nights. By hiding the carcass in cover, there was less chance it would be found by other animals.

Mohini's cub, a male, was now three-quarters grown. He was the survivor of two cubs she had given birth to eighteen months before. He was able to catch his own prey, but he still stayed with Mohini and lived off the food she caught.

After feeding, the two tigers padded quietly along the edge of the forest to drink at a small pool. Then they settled down under the shade of

6

some bushes and slept. When they were not hunting they spent most of their time resting. A herd of deer passed by within a few feet of them. Mohini lifted her head and watched the deer for a moment, but she was too contented to be interested in them and went back to sleep.

With the rainy season at an end, the grass outside the forest was beginning to look brown and parched and food for the grazing animals was becoming scarce. Some of them started to move back into the forest. Soon the tigers would follow them.

▷ Tigers have tongues rougher than sandpaper which they use to rasp at flesh and to clean their fur, stretching and rolling over to reach every patch.

Cleaning up

Mohini and her cub returned to the carcass the following night. Other animals had found their kill but not eaten all the meat. The two tigers enjoyed a good meal, eating more than twenty pounds of meat each. Then they dragged the remains farther into the bushes and covered them with twigs. But the carcass was beginning to smell and to attract scavengers.

With the carcass hidden, the tigers cleaned themselves carefully, using their claws and tongues to comb out dirt and specks of blood from their fur. Only when they felt completely clean did they lie down to sleep again. Generally they slept among the long grass, where their golden-orange coat striped with black was perfect camouflage.

◁ Tigers use any available vegetation or scrape up loose earth to cover a carcass to hide it from other meat-eaters, including other tigers.

The family separates

As the weather became drier and cooler, the tigers moved back into the forest, hunting by stealth among the trees. With no advantage in hunting together, Mohini began to make the cub feel unwelcome. He started to wander by himself. At first he stayed in the same area as Mohini but eventually he left for good. Mohini once again was on her own. Using scent markers, the tigers in the forest spaced themselves out and seldom intruded on each other's area.

▷ Each tiger holds a territory, marking the boundary with strong-smelling urine and dung and with scent deposited on branches and twigs from special glands such as those under its chin. It also warns off other tigers with the occasional roar.

△ Tigers sometimes scratch at trees, both to mark their territory and to remove old, dead, outer layers of their claws.

9

A SOLITARY LIFE

During the cool, dry winter months Mohini roamed through the forests and thickets. She rarely stayed in one place for long, and sometimes traveled many miles in a single night. She tended to keep to paths she had used before, and seldom ventured into areas that were completely unfamiliar. Sometimes she heard a distant roar or could smell where a tiger had passed by, but she avoided the company of other tigers and for weeks did not see one.

As she walked quietly between the bushes and trees, Mohini watched for possible meals. One evening she spotted a small herd of sambar deer. A female deer was at the edge of a clearing, a little apart from the rest. Mohini began to stalk her, moving carefully and never taking her eyes off the animal. Crossing a small opening in the forest, Mohini flattened herself to the ground so the deer would not see her. She paused behind a bush and watched her quarry. Then she crept closer, using the cover of a tree or tuft of grass to remain hidden from view.

As she got within striking distance, she crouched completely still except for the tip of her tail, which twitched nervously. The sambar lifted its head but did not notice Mohini. As it settled to feeding again, Mohini sprang up. With a quick rush she ran at the deer and knocked it down to the ground. Then she grabbed its throat in her powerful jaws. The sambar, unable to breathe, did not put up a struggle and died very quickly. Mohini had made sure of her meals for the next few days.

On the hunt

Mohini was not always so successful when she hunted. Often when she saw a possible victim she would crouch and then spend many minutes carefully stalking the animal only for it to catch wind of her or spot her movement and

move nervously out of range. Sometimes she got as far as making a final rush, only to have the deer or antelope dodge her at the last moment and make off at a speed that Mohini could beat only in a short sprint. An ambush attack was her most successful tactic.

Quenching her thirst

After the hunt Mohini went to drink at a forest pool. She lapped up the water with the back of her tongue. Even at this cool time of year she liked being close to water and occasionally bathed in it to clean her fur.

△▷ Tigers find their prey mainly by sight. They approach carefully and make use of every bit of cover to get as close as possible before making a final high-speed rush. As they pounce, their claws are automatically unsheathed. Only about 1 in 20 of their hunting attempts are successful.

Confrontation

As Mohini wandered through the forest, most other animals moved out of her way in fear. Some birds and monkeys gave alarm calls. Yet she never attacked an animal unless she was hungry. She saved her energy for when she really needed a meal.

A few animals she met were not afraid of tigers. Porcupines arrived to gnaw bones on a carcass she had left. As she approached, one of them rattled its quills. Mohini stood uncertainly, torn between grabbing back the carcass and the memory of a jab from a porcupine's quills when she was younger. Only when the porcupine had finished did she move in.

Mohini lived in an area where people were felling trees to create farmland. She avoided humans, though sometimes she went near roads and villages. Most villagers never suspected that tigers lived so close. Occasionally they heard stories of tigers eating local people but these were rarely true.

▷ Tigers are rarely dangerous to people and, being most active in the early morning or late evening, are not often seen by them.

△ A tiger will usually drive off another animal from a carcass but will treat a porcupine with respect since its quills can inflict nasty wounds.

△ Few animals will attack adult tigers, and while packs of dholes (Indian wild dogs) have been known to do so, a single dhole presents no threat.

At the coolest part of the year Mohini became ready to mate. Her body scent was now attractive to male tigers and they came searching for her. A young male arrived first and approached Mohini warily. She snarled at him and he stopped short but did not go away. But before he could get to know Mohini, an older bigger male arrived. He threatened the young tiger, who recognized that the newcomer was a more powerful animal. The two males scuffled and the smaller one was driven off.

The big male approached Mohini confidently. She growled and snarled and held herself stiffly, torn between the urge to mate and her usual wariness of strangers. She kept snarling, but less strongly, as he came right up to her. Now the two tigers were head to head, whiskers almost touching. The male gently licked Mohini's neck. She lost her fear and moved her head to touch his cheek. Several times she rubbed against him and nipped his fur gently, then turned and moved in front of him. She sank down on her front legs and belly, but kept her back legs slightly raised and lifted her tail. Mohini was ready to mate and the male mounted her.

Mating

The two tigers stayed together for five days and nights. In that time they mated many times. The act of mating lasted only a few seconds. When mounted on Mohini, the male first grabbed the skin on her neck, then gave a high-pitched squeal. Mohini growled and, as they finished mating, she shook him off, striking out with her forepaws. Despite her ferocious appearance she was happy to rest close to the male.

After some minutes the male stood up and approached Mohini again. The tigers greeted one another with low "prruh, prruh" calls. He touched his head to hers and rubbed along her cheek. She responded by rubbing her head and body against him and once again they mated.

Mohini had made a kill the day before the male arrived, and in between matings both tigers went to the carcass and fed. It was then that another male tiger arrived, attracted by Mohini's scent.

▷ When a tigress is "in heat," the special smell of her urine and feces advertises her readiness to mate to males. The whiff makes them wrinkle their lips.

△ Tigers usually mate in winter. When courting and mating, they roar and growl loudly and often. Females are in heat for about 6 days at a time.

△ In her breeding season, a tigress may mate with more than one tiger. At this time, she is less aggressive to other tigers. She presents herself to the male.

Rivalry

The new male was nearly as big as Mohini's mate. Mohini backed away and the two males faced up to one another. Each snarled and showed its fangs, then gave a deep growl. The rivals rocked back on their haunches and shadow-boxed with their front paws. Suddenly the newcomer turned and fled. Mohini's mate took a few steps after him but made no real attempt to catch him.

▷ Tigers' fights are mostly show. The weaker animal is usually allowed to withdraw with no damage done.

Alone again

It was soon after this that the pair lost interest in each other and the male tiger wandered away. Mohini did not see him again all year. For a few days she went into open grassland. The weather was cool but the old dry grass had burned away in the sun. New shoots were springing up. Herds of chital deer were grazing. Mohini tried stalking them but there was not enough cover. She returned to the forest where game was not so plentiful but was easier to approach or ambush.

△ Chital feed on grass but rest among bushes. Tigers find it easier to hunt in cover than in very open country.

17

MOHINI GIVES BIRTH

Towards the end of March the weather started to become warmer, but in the forest there was less cover than before as by now many of the trees had shed their leaves. It was a hard time for Mohini. The reduced cover made stalking more difficult, and she could not avoid rustling the leaves noisily as she walked along. She was in the last few days of her fifteen-week pregnancy and needed plenty of food but, being bulkier and heavier than usual, hunting made her tire very quickly.

Mohini chanced upon a secluded thicket of bushes and bamboo with a tiny clearing in the middle. She made this her home and trampled down the bamboo until she had made a bed of leaves. Here in the den, on the last day of March, she gave birth to her cubs. There were three cubs in the litter and they were all born within an hour. They were tiny compared to their mother and were born blind. They wriggled and cried a little and Mohini carefully cleaned each one with her tongue. She gathered them into one corner of the clearing and lay down close to them. After a couple of hours the cubs wriggled up to her and searched for her teats. One of them was a little smaller than the others and was slow to suckle, but eventually they all found milk. Then, with stomachs full and exhausted by their efforts, the cubs huddled together and slept.

For the first few days of their lives the cubs yearned only for milk and Mohini could not leave them for long.

Feeding her newborn

For almost a week, the tiny tigers were unable to move far, and their eyes stayed closed. But as they grew, they took more milk at each feed and were not so demanding. Mohini was hungry and needed time to hunt.

△ Young tigers grow quickly on their mother's milk and are weaned at about three months. There may be up to six cubs in a litter. Usually only one or two survive beyond a few weeks.

Danger is near

While she was hunting, a hyena came to the den. Mohini could not make a kill and so soon returned. As she approached the den, she saw the hyena run off. Swiftly she checked on her cubs. The smallest had been taken by the hyena. Fearing for the lives of the two other cubs, she moved them one by one to a new den under an overhanging rock on a hillside farther up the valley. Here they could not be seen so easily.

△ Hyenas may take unattended cubs. If a mother tiger senses any danger, she will move her cubs to a safer spot.

△ A tigress carries a cub by holding its head and neck gently between her teeth. The cub is not frightened and keeps still.

◁ Much of the "play" of tiger cubs includes actions the animals will need in adult life. A tigress is tolerant of their games but keeps control on where they go and how much noise they can make.

△ Young cubs need to remain quiet and well hidden when their mother is away. Even once they are eating meat, they are often left hidden during the day while their mother guards a kill nearby.

Keeping the family fed

Moving the cubs and setting up the new den took most of one night. Mohini had now gone several nights without a meal and her milk supplies were low. She set off again to hunt. This time she had more luck, catching a young sambar deer at only her second attempt. She brought her kill back near the den to feed.

With one cub gone, the others, a male and female, now had larger shares of milk and they began to thrive. Soon they started to eat meat. However, Mohini still kept them and the den very clean. She did not allow any blood from a meal or pieces of meat to dirty the cub's fur. She continually licked them clean. When the cubs were tiny, Mohini's licking stimulated them to pass feces and these she cleared away immediately.

As the cubs grew stronger, they moved around more and began to play. They wrestled with one another and sometimes clambered over Mohini. As their movements became less clumsy they began "stalking" one another or pawing at Mohini's tail as she lay twitching it from side to side.

BRINGING UP A FAMILY

As the middle of the year approached, the weather became very hot. More than ever Mohini kept in cover during the heat of the day and made frequent trips to water, both for drinking and bathing. The cubs were too young to be safe in the water yet. Later in the summer Mohini introduced them to water by pulling them into a pool. After the first shock they enjoyed themselves, and like most tigers became good swimmers and especially keen bathers.

By the time they were two months old, the tiger cubs could see well and were beginning to try to follow Mohini, but she did not allow them to travel very far. Living close to the waterhole provided water and also allowed Mohini to see the comings and goings of the deer and wild boar. She managed to get several meals by catching unwary drinkers. Biting her prey by the neck, she took the carcasses to the cubs. Sometimes she removed part of the guts first. Small dead animals she could lift from the ground and walk forward with them to the den but with a large boar or antelope she had to drag the carcass backwards. Then she opened up the skin to allow the cubs to get at the meat.

By the end of June the cubs were used to eating meat. They had grown fast and each weighed about twenty pounds . About this time the surroundings began to change. Although it was still dry and very hot, the woodland trees were beginning to grow leaves again.

Avoiding intruders

While the cubs were young, Mohini was very wary of other animals. On two occasions male tigers passed close by. These tigers moved across a much wider range than female tigers – up to 50 square miles. She took great care to avoid them and watched to see that they did not come too close to the cubs. She regularly marked her territory by spraying urine on bushes.

Mohini spent much of her time on guard, watching over both the cubs and her kills nearby. But on the third occasion she took the cubs on an expedition away from the den, she had a big fright. She was leading the cubs down the track towards the waterhole. As they rounded a corner a male sloth bear stood in the way. Unlike most of the animals Mohini met, he had no fear of tigers. Only when she growled and took a pace forward looking her most threatening did the bear turn aside and move into the undergrowth. Mohini gathered the cubs close to her with a soft deep grunt and carried on down the path.

Near the waterhole she settled down and gave the cubs a reassuring lick. The cubs responded, leaning against Mohini and rubbing their head and shoulders against her. All three tigers purred contentedly.

◁ Tigers vary their facial expressions according to mood. These signal their feelings to other tigers. Their facial markings help make the signals obvious. Expressions such as threat are understood by all animals.

△ Tiger cubs are totally dependent on their mother for their first 18 months. Also in this time they have to learn and perfect the hunting techniques. They go on growing in size until three or four years old. Females mature earlier than males.

Their first hunt

At three months old the cubs had their first hunting lesson. It came about by chance. Walking with the cubs one evening, Mohini spotted a boar grazing in the open. Making the cubs lie down, Mohini began to stalk the boar. Nearer and nearer she crept. The cubs did not know what was going on and were fascinated by the boar and by Mohini's actions.

Just as Mohini got within range, one of the cubs lifted its head to get a better view. The movement alerted the boar, and although Mohini rushed, her quarry was too fast for her. She returned to the cubs, giving an angry cough when she found one of them standing in the open.

Eating together

Later that night, with the cubs safely in the den, Mohini was able to catch a swamp deer and bring it back for the family to feed on. She gripped the carcass with her claws then, with her teeth, peeled back the skin on one side and let the cubs eat before she took her share. They all ate the hindquarters and left the rest for the next night.

△ ▷ The cubs have to learn that to kill a small animal its neck must be broken and a larger animal's throat must be gripped hard to suffocate it.

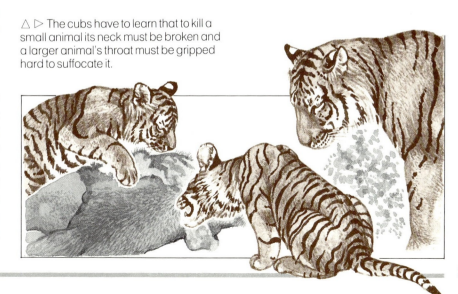

25

THE MONSOON

Early summer saw the rains come to the parched countryside. Shrunken waterholes grew again and lakes filled. The forest, which had looked brown and drab, became green again as leaves grew in profusion and grasses sprouted in the clearings and open spaces. But for many of the animals the forest became an uncomfortable place. It was very hot and damp and heavy rain drops constantly dripped on them from the tree leaves. Mosquitoes hummed under the tree canopy and leeches waited to fasten onto an unsuspecting host. The chital, wild boar, and many of the other animals moved to grassland or open forest. Here breezes made the air a little cooler and there were fewer insects to annoy them.

Mohini and her cubs moved out of their den, which was now dank and inhospitable, and followed the herds into the open forest. From time to time Mohini still left the cubs in a thicket when she went to hunt, but now they could follow her quite easily. They no longer had a need for a permanent home and started to live as adults, constantly on the move in search of food.

Mohini began to train the cubs in the art of hunting. To begin with they were hopelessly clumsy, but as time went on their technique improved. It would be months, though, before they caught their own food. Even when they would be well over a year old Mohini would still capture most of the prey, usually sitting back while the cubs satisfied their large appetites before eating her own meal.

In the open country the tigers were sometimes noticed by the other animals. Langur monkeys spied them from above and gave their alarm call, so alerting other creatures. But Mohini usually found enough cover for her striped camouflage to conceal her, and the family made a good living from the grasslands during the monsoon rains. Later when the rains ended, prey and predators, including Mohini and the cubs, would move back into the forest.

Trial and error

The cubs began to experiment with hunting for themselves. By the time they were five months old Mohini allowed them to wander 130 to 150 feet from her, and they sometimes practiced creeping up on a small animal such as a peafowl or deer fawn. Their stalking action was good but they always seemed to fail when it came to the final rush at their target. They were either too eager or too cautious. Mohini continued to train them to make a kill.

Learning to kill

Mohini brought down a gazelle and disabled it so that it could not run. She allowed the cubs to try to kill it, using their teeth and claws, but they dealt with the animal clumsily, and she had to kill it for the family to feed. However, they soon developed the technique of seizing a prey's neck or throat. The cubs began to assist their mother in hunting, the three tigers working together as a team, but Mohini always made sure of killing or disabling large prey so that the youngsters were not injured in a struggle.

△ Cubs have hunting instincts but need to learn to wait for prey to come close and to stalk rather than chase their quarry.

△ Small animals such as frogs, reptiles, and birds are often the target for a cub's hunting. All tigers will also eat carrion.

Camp followers

Mohini usually guarded fresh carcasses well. There were always other large predators, such as hyenas and jackals, ready to feed on a tiger kill if they got the chance. Several types of vulture were also waiting to swoop on unattended carcasses.

It had been a good summer for Mohini. She had been able to provide enough food to rear two healthy cubs and she had put on weight again. But it would be another whole year before the cubs would become independent and she could again live a solitary life.

◁ To survive, an adult tiger needs to kill and eat a large animal such as a sambar about once a week. A tiger may eat 30 pounds of meat in one meal but there are many days when it eats nothing.

CONSERVATION

The tiger has suffered greatly at the hands of humans. Enormous numbers of tigers have been killed, either for "sport" or to provide fur coats or rugs. Even though strict laws now govern fur trading in many parts of the world, there are still places where furs are traded, legally or illegally. Until no one is prepared to pay to wear tiger fur, the animal will always be in danger.

The tiger is a possible danger to people and their livestock, although it rarely attacks either if it can find wild prey. But in places such as India the human population has expanded into the wild forests. Tigers have been seen as a threat and have often been trapped or poisoned simply because they *might* be dangerous.

In reality we have no idea just how many tigers there once were. One estimate suggests there were 30,000 tigers in India 50 years ago. Now there are only about 2,500. Tigers have disappeared entirely from the Indonesian island of Bali, and other races of tiger such as the Siberian and Sumatran are very scarce. The world population of tigers is estimated to be little more than 4,000.

Protection is vital if the tiger is to survive. In India shooting has been banned since 1970, and the export of skins since 1968. Some areas have been set aside as tiger reserves and in these the environment is protected. The tiger is a very adaptable animal, able to live in forests, grassland, and swamps, and when it is not persecuted it can hold its own or increase.

For more information
Useful information about tiger conservation can be obtained from the World Wildlife Fund, 1601 Connecticut Ave. N.W., Washington, D.C. 20009.

▷ This tiger has been sedated using a dart gun. It has been fitted with a radio collar so its movements can be followed.

Photo: Lee Lyon, Survival Anglia

Fact file

Tigers in the far north of their range experience very cold winters. In the tropics it is usually warm but even so the weather affects tigers' behavior. In central India, where our tiger lives, it is dry for much of the year, but heavy monsoon rains occur in the summer, changing the vegetation and the tiger's routine.

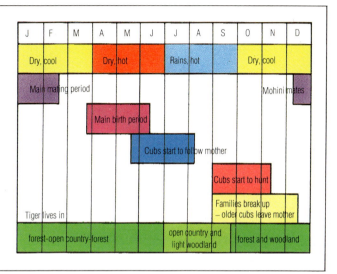

J	F	M	A	M	J	J	A	S	O	N	D
Dry, cool			Dry, hot		Rains, hot				Dry, cool		
Main mating period										Mohini mates	
			Main birth period								
					Cubs start to follow mother						
									Cubs start to hunt		
									Families break up – older cubs leave mother		
Tiger lives in forest-open country-forest					open country and light woodland				forest and woodland		

Index